AF374805

Stop, Luke!

Written by

Erin Johnson

Illustrated by

Emily Hercock

Dedicated to my younger brothers, Junior and Luke.

My little brother, Luke, makes too much noise.

He loses all my
things...

And he ruins
all my toys.

He wakes me up
in the middle of
the night.

He eats all my
snacks...

WHAM
BAM
K-POW!

And he loves to fight.

He tore out pages
from the books
we've read.

Luke messes up my drawings...

And he jumps on
my bed.

Stop, Luke!
STOP, LUKE!
STOP, LUKE!

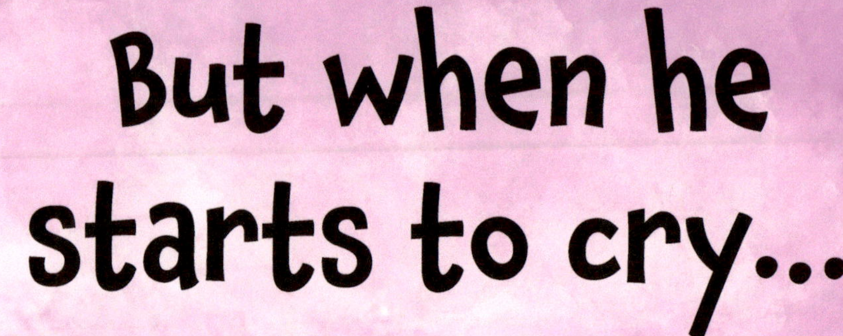

But when he
starts to cry...

Aww...

I let out a
big sigh.

We sit on my rug,
and I give him a hug.

Because although Luke can do very annoying things, I still love him so much.